PRAC

A CONTEMPORARY INTERPRETATION
OF THE WORDS OF NICHOLAS HERMAN
(BROTHER LAWRENCE c.1614–1691)

THE

PRESENCE

OF GOD

MARK BILTON

MONDAY
matters

A Monday Matters
Publication

"I first encountered Brother Lawrence as a new Christian some 40 years ago. How special to see this classic brought into the 21st century—and especially at the hand of my friend, Mark Bilton. I know of no more practical way to eliminate the false sacred-secular division that plagues believers in the business world, than to come back daily to the simple reality, so well taught by Brother Lawrence, that God is as present with us at work as in the prayer closet."

MIKE BAER, CHIEF PEOPLE OFFICER, EMPLOYBRIDGE USA, INTERNATIONAL SPEAKER AND AUTHOR OF 'BUSINESS AS MISSION'.

"This amazing little book by Brother Lawrence is one of the great classics of Christian literature. And rightly so, as this young priest who worked in often drab and difficult circumstances, so glowed with the very Presence of God. That Mark Bilton has taken the time to bring this jewel into the 21st Century by making it accessible to a whole new generation is an incredible blessing."

BERNI DYMET, INTERNATIONAL RADIO PERSONALITY, AUTHOR, SPEAKER AND CEO CHRISTIANITY WORKS.

"Every day the Lord has made. Yes, every day; so who better to spend time with every day? Spending time in the presence of God opens the door to God ideas for our business, careers and life. Mark has experienced 'Presence of God' ideas, and so have I."

PETER IRVINE, CO FOUNDER GLORIA JEAN'S COFFEES AUSTRALIA, AUTHOR AND SPEAKER.

"If you want to understand how to integrate faith and work, then Mark's books are a must read. You will learn the tools to success and fruitfulness without compromising your integrity."

ALEX COOK, FOUNDER AND EXECUTIVE DIRECTOR, WEALTH WITH PURPOSE.

"An inspiring book from an inspiring man! Mark Bilton has left behind footprints on this earth—and you can see where he has walked. Thank you for your generosity and valuable insights."

STEVEN P BENNETT OAM, FOUNDER, BENBRO ELECTRONICS, AND AUTHOR OF 'MORE THAN A CONQUEROR'.

Called to Business
19 Delaware Avenue,
St Ives NSW 2075 AUSTRALIA
Telephone +61 2 99880956
www.CalledtoBusiness.com

Except where otherwise indicated in the text, the Scripture quotations contained herein are from The Holy Bible, New International Version®, NIV® Copyright © 1973, 1978, 1984, 2011 by Biblica, Inc.™ Used by permission. All rights reserved worldwide.

Cataloguing in Publication Data:
Title: PRACTICE the Presence of God. A Contemporary Interpretation of the Words of Nicholas Herman / Mark Bilton
ISBN: 9780987339843 (paperback)
ISBN: 9780987339898 (ebook)
Subjects: Religion and Theology, Business and Economic
Dewey Number: 248.4

Cover & Layout Design by Justine Elliott – Book Layout Guru

"Rejoice always, pray continually, give thanks in all circumstances; for this is God's will for you in Christ Jesus.

(1 THESSALONIANS 5:16 - 18)

CONTENTS

ACKNOWLEDGMENTS

There are many who acknowledge Jesus as Saviour, some who serve Him as Lord, but few who walk daily in full communion with Him. In my life there are two people I know who literally 'walk the talk' and 'practice the presence of God'.

To my good friend Ian Harry, you are a consistent example of one who communes with God, and have a walk I continue to endeavour to emulate.

To Ian's mentor and my acquaintance, Pastor Fergus McIntyre, thank you for making this message of 'The Presence' your life's work, you are an encouragement and example to all you meet.

Lastly my thanks to John Ignatius Wareham Paterson, without your expertise and diligence this book would not have been created. Your appreciation and interpretation of the original French text were paramount in ensuring the nuances of the original writer's intent were maintained.

INTRODUCTION

The *Practice of the Presence of God* is a revered and venerated collection of conversations and letters that capture the wisdom and simple message of Brother Lawrence of the Resurrection. This fresh contemporary version is an attempt to reintroduce his much-needed message.

With that at the forefront of my mind I have endeavoured in introduce it to a new generation. I have been careful to honour the original and yet make it assessable and applicable to a digital world. The truth is timeless; as relevant now to our walk with God as it was in the 17th Century. It is a discipline that has been lost and needs to be embraced once again.

Nicholas Herman's message was simple yet utterly profound. The discipline of being cognisant of God's presence and serving in utter reliance on Him is at the core of what it means to be a follower of Jesus.

My passion and purpose is to see Christians in the workplace be effective for God and to see His plans and purposes worked out in their vocations. In order to do that we need to know that God has a plan for us that includes our work. We have to be obedient to his calling and to his Word. To be obedient we have to hear, and to hear we have to 'practice the presence of God' and walk in close communion with Him. Then and only then is He Lord and His Kingdom established in the workplace.

The concept that God is vitally, passionately, and intimately interested in our workplace, our business, or our place of employment is completely foreign to most of us. We, 'the church', the collective body of Christ, have fallen into a misconception. One that seems innocuous and unimportant. We have segmented our lives into that which is sacred and that which is secular. This separation has rendered us relatively impotent in reaching and impacting our world for the Kingdom of God.

We spend more time at work than anywhere else. The Psalmist says that: "All the days ordained for me were written in your book before one of then came to be." (Psa 139:16) God has a plan for our Monday as well as our Sunday.

Work was a part of God's plan enacted before the fall in a perfect world. "The Lord God took the man and put him in the Garden of Eden to work it and take care of it" (Gen 2:15). What we sometimes consider mundane and menial is ordained and designed by God. We are called to engage with our Creator in the midst of our labour. "Whatever your task works at it heartily as for the lord and not for men." (Col 3:23)

God has ordained each one to work in alignment with our unique gifting and His call; "Each one of you should retain the place in life that the Lord assigned to him and to which he called him. (1 Cor 7:17)

There is no such thing as secular employment for the believer. Once we are born again, everything about us is redeemed for Kingdom purposes. Every believer is in fulltime ministry, only a few have pulpits in sanctuaries. Embrace your call with the faithfulness and thankfulness worthy of the One who has called you.

My desire is to see businesspeople all over the world released into the freedom and knowledge of God's plan and purpose in the workplace. With revelation and empowerment, potential is released and dreams are realized. God has a plan and a purpose for your life, and it has been my experience that, without exception, we are all anointed and appointed for a specific purpose.

May I encourage you to take the simple message in this book and apply it to your life. You will find God in the midst of the mundane and the seemingly meaningless and you will be building His Kingdom as you do.

BIOGRAPHY OF
NICHOLAS HERMAN

Brother Lawrence, was born Nicholas Herman in Herimenil, Lorraine, France, in 1614.

He lived during the tumultuous Early Modern period of European history. It was almost 100 years since Martin Luther nailed his famous document to the church door in Wittenberg. Europe was storming with the conflict between Protestant and Catholic, brutally manifest in the "Thirty Year War". Louis XIV was Nicholas' king.

The Black Plague was common, notably in the 1665 Great Plague of London and the subsequent Great Fire. Yet in the cauldron of change were birthed great minds and brave souls who have stood the crucible of history. Harvard was founded in 1636, and great authors like Bunyan and composers such as Bach gave us timeless classics. There was a thought revolution in the religious and scientific communities whose champions were the likes of Bacon, Descartes, Newton and Pascal.

Nicholas was born into obscurity to a poor family of little means. He had little education other than from his local parish priest Lawrence. He had an influential Uncle, Jean Majeur, who was a member of the Discalced Carmelites.

In 1629 Nicholas enlisted in the military during the worst period of the "Thirty Year War (1618-1648). History does not tell us why he joined the army, but it was common practice and often required for those of low means to serve their nation in this way. For some it was the only means of survival.

Whilst serving at war, he had a revelation of God that would impact him forever. Characteristically, it was an ordinary sight not a supernatural manifestation.

It was winter, when Herman saw a completely barren tree; it looked in its dormant state, for all purposes, dead and lifeless. Yet it seemed to wait with expectation for the new season and the new leaves, fruit and life that would come.

He now understood God's grace and the sovereignty of His divine providence. He identified with the tree, lifeless and dormant, but God had more for him, and the season of Spring would eventuate. With that revelation from the Spirit of God, in an everyday experience, "he was struck by a vision of God's power and providence so strong that it would remain forever in his soul."

He found God in the mundane and the ordinary; something that would mark him and those who have been influenced by him. But his life was about to take another unexpected turn. Some scholars believe he was captured by the Germans, threatened with execution and let go, but then subsequently injured by the Swedes at Rambervillers. He was wounded in 1635 with a near fatal injury to his sciatic nerve, an affiliation that would leave him impaired and in chronic pain for the remainder of his life.

Nicholas then returned home and after a period of recovery served for period as a footman for M. de Fuibert the Treasurer of the Exchequer. He described himself as one, "who was clumsy and broke everything". Obviously he was ill suited for such a role.

In 1640 Nicholas Herman entered The Order of The Brothers of Our Lady of Mount Carmel, (Carmelite) monastery in Paris. He was given or took the name of his uncle and became: Brother Lawrence of the Resurrection.

Carmelite spirituality is based in the 'Vita Apostolica' movement of the 12th and 13th centuries and came to prominence in the 16th century Spanish Reformation, and 17th century France. Rooted in incarnational spirituality, Carmelites served by imitating Christ and the disciples in radical poverty.

The Order of Carmelites has its origins, as you would imagine, on Mount Carmel. This was where the Prophet Elijah defeated the priests of Baal (1 Kings 18), by demonstrating who the true God was. In the 12th century after the 3rd Crusade some European pilgrims came to Mount Carmel, to live as hermits like Elijah, and the Carmelite Movement was born.

Brother Lawrence served there for fifteen years as a cook, and then worked in the sandal repair shop serving up to one hundred friars. But he never stopped helping in the busy kitchen, and was often called back to serve in his original capacity.

It was amidst the tedious chores of cooking and cleaning in the mundane and menial that he developed his 'best rule of Holy life'. He describes this in his own words; "Men invent means and methods of coming at God's love, they learn rules and set up devices to remind them of that love, and it seems like a world of trouble to bring oneself into the consciousness of God's presence. Yet it might be so simple. Is it not quicker and easier just to do our common business wholly for the love of him?"

It was not the task but the motivation and the experience of God in the midst of the task that made it profound, made it sacred, made it holy. He broke the barrier between the sacred and the secular, all at once finding unity of spirituality and experience, a life wholly surrendered to God.

"The time for work is no different from the time for prayer: in the noise and clutter of my kitchen, when different people are calling me about different things, all at the same time, I feel God's presence with the same tranquility as when I kneel to receive Communion."

So profound was this revelation it became his single focus. One that demanded a lot of discipline and he struggled with it for years.

"I worshipped Him as often as I could, keeping the thought of His presence always in my mind, and reminding myself of it as soon as I found my mind straying from Him. I found this exercise very far from easy, yet I persisted in it, through all my difficulties, without worrying or becoming troubled when my mind had wandered despite itself. I made this my business, not just at the times appointed for prayer, but all day long, at all times, every hour, every minute, even in the busiest periods of my work, I drove from my mind every thought which could possibly distract me from thinking of God."

It was only when he reconciled himself to the struggle and his destiny that he found peace. Nicholas Herman, Brother Lawrence of the Resurrection, found ultimate peace when he passed into the arms of his beloved Saviour in 1691.

We have the legacy of his revelation, struggle and experience, simply painted for us in a collection of conversations and letters. Father Joseph de Beaufort, later Vicar General of Cardinal de Noailles, documented four conversations that he had with Brother Lawrence. Those conversations and Herman's own letters form what we know as 'The Practice of The Presence of God'. De Beaufort also wrote Nicholas' eulogy in which we glean more of this man's life and walk with God.

In this modern version of that classic collection, Nicholas Herman shows us how to commune in the common-place. How to live in the now and be mindful of God in the moment, to live from the heart and not always from the head.

He left us a priceless gift, a way to live life regardless of vocation, circumstance or age; A way to commune with our Creator and experience His Peace, His Love and His Presence.

Having been birthed in the awful conflicts and atrocities of the 'Thirty Year War' it is a beautiful irony that 'The Practice of The Presence of God' became recognized and venerated by Catholic and Protestant Denominations alike, and its proponents include John Wesley and A. W. Tozer.

"The time for work is no different from the time for prayer: in the noise and clutter of my kitchen, when different people are calling me about different things, all at the same time, I feel God's presence with the same tranquility as when I kneel to receive Communion."

NICHOLAS HERMAN
(BROTHER LAWRENCE C.1605 - 1691)

FIRST
CONVERSATION

3RD AUGUST 1666

I MET BROTHER LAURENCE FOR THE FIRST TIME ON 3RD August, 1666. It was then that he told me of the great favour God had shown him when he was eighteen, at the moment of his conversion.

It was Winter, and as he looked at a bare tree, and thought of how, when Spring came, first its leaves, and then its fruit and its flowers, would grow back, he was struck by a vision of God's power and providence so strong that it would remain forever in his soul. He could not say whether, in all the forty years since, it had ever grown stronger than it was that day.

He told me that as the treasurer, M. Fieubert's, footman, he was always breaking things in his clumsiness. He had asked to take religious orders so as to sacrifice his life and his pleasures to God, for he was certain he would be made to suffer for this awkwardness and for the faults he would commit there. And yet God had disappointed him: he had known only satisfaction there.

He told me also that we must put ourselves in constant communion with God, so as always to feel his presence within us. It was shameful to leave this communion for trivial and foolish thoughts. Rather, we should keep our souls constantly fed with high thoughts of God, if we were to gain the joy which comes from devotion.

It was our faith, he said, which we must quicken and enliven. It was faith which was the spirit of the Church, faith alone which could lead us close to perfection if we followed it as a rule of conduct—and yet it was too often forgotten and ignored, replaced by trivial devotions which changed every day.

We must abandon ourselves entirely to God, both in our temporal and spiritual lives, and be happy that we were doing His will. Whether this was in suffering or in consolation should make no difference to a man of true submission. We needed to show our faithfulness in these dark, cold and arid moments where God was testing our love for Him: just a single act of resignation in such moments could bring us a lot further along our path to Him.

Every day he would hear accounts of the suffering which was caused by sin, and yet far from being astonished by them, he was rather surprised that they were not more frequent, for he knew what sinners were capable of. He prayed for them, but did not trouble himself further, for he knew that God could make right all the wrong they did.

He told me that to abandon ourselves to God fully, as He wishes us to, we must keep a careful watch over every one of our passions, from the most spiritual to the most worldly and base: he said that God would guide through these passions anyone who truly desired to serve him. If this was my aim in life too, to serve God truly, I could come to him, Brother Laurence, as often as I wished, and need not worry about disturbing him; but if it was not my aim, he did not wish to see me again.

SECOND CONVERSATION

28TH SEPTEMBER 1666

HE TOLD ME THAT HE HAD LET LOVE RULE everything he did, and not any selfish concerns; and that, in taking God's love as his one aim in every action he undertook, he had never been disappointed. He was happy to pick up a straw from the ground for the love of God, for Him alone and nothing else, not even for His gifts.

He said he had been greatly troubled by the thought that he must certainly be damned, and that he could not have been convinced otherwise even by everyone else in the world. Yet he reasoned to himself: "I have entered into the religious life for one reason, the love of God, and have sought to act for Him alone. Whether I am damned or saved, this is my aim, to act purely for His love. I will at least have the merit of having done everything I could to love Him, even until my death."

He had been troubled like this for four years, four years in which he had suffered greatly. But he finally came to see that this trouble was the result of his own lack of faith, and ever since he lived his life perfectly freely, and was always joyful. He would place his sins between himself and God, as if to tell Him that he did not deserve the graces he received, and yet that did not stop God from continuing to rain these gifts down on him.

He told me that, to cultivate the habit of continual communion with God, we must at first come to Him with everything we had done, but that, after a little time, our effort would be rewarded and we would have no difficulty in feeling His love awake within us.

He said that he had expected, after the good times God had given him, to have his share of troubles and of suffering, but this thought did not worry him, for he knew well that, as he was capable of nothing on his own, God would not fail to give him the strength he would need to bear them.

Whenever life presented him with an opportunity for practising a virtue, he would always turn to God, and say to Him, "God, I cannot do this unless you give me strength", and then God would always give him the strength he needed, and more besides.

Whenever he failed in his duty, he would never do otherwise than to confess his fault, and to say to God, "This is all I will ever do, if you leave me to my own devices: it is you who must stop me from falling, and correct what is amiss, for I am absolutely committed to following you." And then he worried no more about it, for he knew that he had made his peace with God.

He told me that we must act towards God with great simplicity, speak to Him with great frankness, and ask for His help as soon as we felt the need for it. He would never fail to give it to us, and he knew that from experience.

Why, it was not long ago that he had been sent to Burgundy to buy the provision of wine for the order. He found this a very onerous task, for not only did he have no skill for business deals, but he was also lame in one leg. Indeed, the only way he was able to walk around the boat was by rolling himself over the casks. But he worried himself neither about this, nor about the purchase of the wine: he simply told God that this was His business he was doing, and then he found that everything took care of itself, and took care of itself well.

He had been sent to Auvergne the previous year for the same reason, and though he could not remember how, he knew that his work had been done well, and that it was not he who had done it.

He had found the same thing in his work in the kitchen, the task for which he had the greatest natural aversion. He had developed the habit of dedicating all his work there to God and, by asking Him on each occasion to grant him His grace as he did His work, he had never had the slightest difficulty, not in all the fifteen years he had been assigned there.

He was now working as a cobbler, and very pleased with that post, but he would be happy to leave that job as he had left those before it, so long as, whatever his position might be, he was doing little things for the love of God.

For him the set times of prayer were no different from any other times: he would retire to pray when instructed to by his Superior, but he neither desired nor sought out these times. His greatest labours did not distance him from God. He knew that he must love God in all things, and did his best to do so: he had no need of a director to guide him, but rather of a confessor to absolve him of his sins. He was very conscious of his faults, but he did not let them discourage him: he admitted them to God, without making any plea for forgiveness, and then, at peace with himself and God, resumed his exercise of love and of adoration.

When he was troubled, he turned to nobody for help, but guided only by the light of faith and the knowledge that God was present, he contented himself with acting always for Him, with the sole desire of pleasing Him, come what may.

He said it was futile thoughts which ruin everything, and that that is where evil starts, but we should be careful to reject any thought which we see has no use either for the task in hand, or for our salvation, and to return to our communion with God.

At first, he had often spent the time assigned to prayer rejecting these wandering thoughts and then falling back into them. He had never been able to regulate his devotion as others did: he found that acts of penitence and other exercises were only useful in as much as they helped bring about a union with God through love. He had given this careful thought, and found that it was even quicker to go straight to Him, in a continual exercise of love, doing everything for the love of God.

He said that we must distinguish well between acts of understanding and acts of will: the first made little difference, and the others, all the difference. Our only aim in life must be to love and rejoice in God. No possible act of penitence, if it were separated from love, could ever remove a single sin. We must await the remission of our sins through the blood of Jesus Christ, without worrying, but only striving to love him with all our hearts: he said that God seemed to choose the greatest sinners for his greatest favours, so as more powerfully to show his mercy.

He told me that the greatest pains and pleasures of this world could not be compared with those he had experienced in a spiritual state, and so he cared for nothing and feared nothing, asking only one thing of God, that he might not offend Him. He was not beset by guilt or self-doubt, saying that if he failed in his duty, he admitted it freely, saying he could not do otherwise, if left to his own devices; whereas if he did not fail, he gave thanks to God, knowing that the merit was His.

THIRD CONVERSATION

22ND NOVEMBER 1666

H E TOLD ME THAT HE HAD FOUNDED HIS spiritual life on a high notion and esteem for God in faith. Once this idea had become fully formed, he had had no other care than to reject from the very beginning any other thought, and to carry out all his actions for the love of God. When he had spent what was sometimes a long time without thinking of Him, he did not trouble himself about it. Yet when he had admitted his wretchedness to God, he came back to Him with so much more trust in his goodness that it made him feel still more wretched to have forgotten Him.

He said that this trust which we place in God honours Him greatly and earns us great favours.

It was impossible not only for God to deceive us, but also for Him to let any soul suffer for long, if that soul has submitted itself fully to his will, and resolved to endure anything for his sake. He had succeeded in becoming free of all thoughts, save for thoughts of God. He had known God to come promptly to his aid so often, that when he had business to do, he gave no thought to it beforehand, but when the time came when he must act, he found in God, as in a clear mirror, all that he needed to do in that moment. He had acted like this for some time, without anticipating problems, whereas before that experience, he had used planning and foresight. When he was distracted from God by thoughts of external business, his soul would be enflamed by a fresh memory coming from God, and he would find it difficult to contain his joy. Indeed, he felt much more united with God in his everyday activities, than he did when he retired for his spiritual exercises.

He expected to suffer in the future some great bodily or mental pain: the worst which could befall him would be to lose that sense of God which he had had for so long, but God's goodness made him sure that He would never leave him entirely, and that He would give him the strength to bear any evil He would allow to befall him. With this thought, he had no more fears and did not need to unburden his soul to anyone. When he had tried to do so, he had always ended up more troubled than he had been before. Knowing he was ready to lay down his life for the love of God, he had no fear of danger. Perfect submission to God's will was a path which lead surely to Heaven, and a path which there was always enough light to guide us along.

He said that, when we first started along this path to the spiritual life, we must be faithful in doing our duty and in self-denial, but that, after this, words could not express how great our pleasure would be. In moments of difficulty, we need only have recourse to Jesus Christ, and ask for His grace, and all would be made easy.

He told me that many stopped at penances, or at exercises of their own, while neglecting the love of God, which is their end, and that this could be clearly seen in their works, and explained why these were of no real merit.

Neither art nor science were needed to reach God, he said, but only a heart determined to give itself over to none but Him, and to love no other but Him.

FOURTH
CONVERSATION

25TH NOVEMBER 1666

H E SPOKE TO ME OFTEN, AND VERY OPENLY, about the way in which he approached God, which I have already started to discuss. He told me that it is not by renouncing everything we know in this world that we become closer to God, but only by remaining in continual communion with him, and this could be done quite freely and simply. We need only recognise His presence within us, call on Him constantly, ask for His guidance where we are unsure what His will is, and His help in doing what we know to be His will, offer up all these actions to Him, and thank Him when they are completed.

He said that this conversation with God was also an act of praise, adoration and love for His infinite goodness and perfection.

We should also pray for His grace with complete confidence of receiving it, as the Lord's goodness and mercy were infinite. He said that God never failed to offer us His grace, and that he himself knew this very well, for the only times he had not received God's grace had been those times when he had forgotten to ask for it, or where his thoughts had strayed from an awareness of God's presence. God would always guide us through our doubts, so long as our only aim was to please Him.

Salvation, he said, did not depend on what work we did, but on doing it for God's sake, rather than for our own. He had known too many people who had mistaken the means for the end, and had set about compulsively doing certain kinds of work, only to do it very badly, because of their human and selfish concerns.

He found that the best way to approach God was to go about our daily business purely (as far as we could) for his love, and without any thought for pleasing men: we should act as Paul had instructed us in Galatians, 1:10, and Ephesians, 6:5-6. The idea that times of prayer should be treated differently to other times was a great delusion: we had as great an obligation to be faithful to God through action, in times which called for action, as we did through prayer, when it was time for prayer.

His own act of prayer consisted of nothing else but feeling God's presence, so that his soul was emptied of every sensation but for the sensation of Divine love. When the assigned times for prayer were over, it did not feel any different to him: he continued praising God and blessing him with all his might, so that his life was always joyful. He only hoped that God would make him suffer a little, so as to make him stronger.

Now, he said, was the time to put all our trust in God

alone, once and for all, and surrender ourselves entirely to Him, knowing that He would not deceive us.

He said that we should not tire of doing little things for the love of God, because God does not see how big or small an action is, but only the love with which it is performed. Nor should we be surprised if we often failed in our efforts at first: with time we would develop a habit which would allow us to perform them perfectly, to our complete satisfaction, without even knowing how we had done so.

He told me that religion's whole essence is faith, hope and love, which bring those who practice them into union with God: everything else was important only a means to the end of faith, hope and love, with which it would merge and fade away. Anything is possible to those who believe, less difficult to those who hope, easier to those who love, and still easier to those who persist in all these virtues.

So the aim we must give ourselves is to be the most perfect worshippers of God we can possibly be in this life, as we hope to be throughout all eternity.

When we begin building this spiritual life, we should first make a careful examination of what we are. And this should show us that we are quite contemptible creatures, such as do not deserve the name of Christians: we are at the mercy of all kinds of miseries, and troubled by numberless accidents, in our health, in our state of mind, indeed in our whole inner and outer makeup. All in all, we could see that we were people God would humble with many troubles, both internal and external. And so we should not then be surprised to come up against troubles, temptations, contradictions or opposing thoughts from the world of men. Rather, we should submit to them and bear them for as long as God pleases, knowing that this is for our own good and that they can help us a great deal.

The more perfect a soul seeks to be, he said, the more dependant it is on Divine grace.

When a member of his own order (one he had no choice but to be open with), asked him how he had come to feel God's presence so strongly and so often, he replied that ever since he had first arrived in the monastery, he had seen God as the end of all his thoughts and desires, the point to which they should lean towards, and finish at. At the start of his novitiate, he spent the time assigned for private prayer thinking of God: he nurtured this thought so as to establish the knowledge of God's existence not only as a firm conviction in his mind, but also as an impression deeply engraved upon his heart. He arrived at this knowledge not by any learned or elaborate reasoning, but rather by feelings of devotion, and submission to the light of faith. It was this simple, reliable method which he used to keep himself practiced in the knowledge and the love of God: he did his utmost to be always conscious of His presence and, if he could, never to forget Him again.

When he finished his prayers, his mind filled with great thoughts of that infinite Being, he went to the work assigned him in the kitchen (he was cook to the order). There he thought first of each individual task his work required, then of how and when it should be done, and spent any time which remained, whether before or after his work, in prayer.

When he first started work, he would say to God, trusting Him like a son, "Dear God, as you are with me, and as if I am to obey Your will I must now apply my mind to these outward things, I beg you to allow me the grace of remaining in your presence: and I ask that you help me to achieve that end, and that you accept all my work, and all my affection as yours alone."

As he went on with his work, he also continued his familiar conversation with his Maker, begging for His grace, and offering all his actions up to Him.

When he had finished, he examined his conscience, asking himself how well he had done his duty: if he thought he had succeeded, he gave thanks to God; if not, he asked his forgiveness, but he was not discouraged, he put his mind back in order, and returned to his exercise of God's presence as though he had never left it. "It is like this", he said, "by picking myself up when I fall down, and by constantly repeated acts of faith and love, that I have reached a point where it would now be more difficult for me not to think of God, as it was for me to first become accustomed to His presence.

It was natural for Brother Laurence to urge others to walk in the presence of God, given the great help that it had been to him, but his example did more to persuade people than any argument he could give them. Anyone who so much as looked at his face could not fail to be moved by the sweet and calm devotion which was written on it. And it could be seen that, however busy he was, however much hurry there might be in the kitchen, he always remained calm, his thoughts focussed on Heaven. He neither rushed nor loitered, but did everything at the proper time, and always with the same calmness and equanimity. "For me", he said, "the time for work is no different from the time for prayer: in the noise and clutter of my kitchen, when different people are calling me about different things, all at the same time, I feel God's presence with the same tranquillity as when I kneel to receive Communion."

FIRST LETTER

WRITTEN ON AN UNKNOWN DATE

My Dear Brother,

As it means so much to you that I should explain to you the method by which I succeeded in keeping always in my mind that sense of God's presence which our Lord, in His mercy, had the goodness to grant me, I must tell you that I do so only with great difficulty, and on the condition that you show this letter to nobody. If I thought that you would let others see it, then however much I care about your progress, I could not bring myself to write it. This much I can tell you: I found many books with different methods for approaching God, and various spiritual exercises, but I thought that these would be more likely to confuse me than to help me achieve my goal, which was none other than to become wholly one with God.

And so I resolved to give my all for the Almighty: so after I gave myself wholly to God, so as to do what I could to atone for my sins, I gave up, for the sake of His love alone, everything which was not Him, and began to act as though there were nobody but He and I left in the world. Sometimes, when I addressed him, I felt like a poor criminal before a judge, while at other times I saw him in my heart as my Father, my God. I worshipped Him as often as I could, keeping the thought of His presence always in my mind, and reminding myself of it as soon as I found my mind straying from Him. I found this exercise very far from easy, yet I persisted in it, through all my difficulties, without worrying or becoming troubled when my mind had wandered despite itself. I made this my business, not just at the times appointed for prayer, but all day long, at all times, every hour, every minute, even in the busiest periods of my work, I drove from my mind every thought which could possibly distract me from thinking of God.

This is the practice I have always followed, ever since I started out in the religious life, and although I have done it very far from perfectly, I have found it to be of great benefit. This, I know, is due wholly to the goodness and mercy of God, because without Him we can do nothing, and I least of all. But when we keep ourselves faithfully in His presence, and put ourselves always before Him, not only can we never offend Him, at least not deliberately, but we also gain a holy freedom, and if I may put it in these terms, a familiarity with God, whom we may ask for all the graces we need, knowing that we will receive them. In short, by constantly repeating these acts, they become habitual, and God's presence begins to seem natural to us. Please join me in thanking Him for His great goodness towards me, which I can never admire enough, and for the many favours He has granted to so miserable a sinner as I. May all things praise Him. Amen.

I am yours in our Lord,

SECOND LETTER
WRITTEN PRIOR TO NOVEMBER 1685

My Dear Reverend,

As I can find nothing about my way of life in books, although it presents no difficulty to me, I should like to know your thoughts about it, so that I can be the more sure on whether I am following the right path.

Some days ago I was speaking with a pious man, who told me that the spiritual life was a life of grace, which begins with servile fear, grows with the hope of eternal life, and arrives in its fullness with pure love: he said that each of these states of mind had its different stages, by which that blessed end is finally reached.

Yet, far from following all these methods, I cannot say what instinct it was which told me that they would serve only to discourage me. That was the reason why, when I first took religious orders, I resolved to give myself up to God, as the best atonement I could make for my sins, and for love of Him, to renounce all other things.

During my early years in the monastery, I often spent the time assigned for devotion thinking of death, Judgement, Heaven, Hell and my sins. I carried on like this for some years, spending all the rest of the day, even the times when I was busiest with work, applying my mind carefully to the presence of God: I always considered Him to be with me, and often to be in me.

Much later, I began, without quite realising what was happening, to do the same thing during the time assigned to me for prayer, and this was a great joy and consolation to me. This practice gave me such a high regard for God that faith alone could satisfy me on that point.*

It was like this that I started out, yet I must tell you that I suffered a good deal in those first ten years: from the fear that I was not as devoted to God as I wished to be, from my past sins which were never far from my mind, and from the great undeserved favours which God did to me. I often fell during this time, but did not fail to rise again after each fall. It seemed to me that reason, God Himself and all His Creation were against me, and that faith alone was for me. I was sometimes troubled by the thought that it was presumptuous of me to believe that I had received such favours, that I was presuming to already be at a point which others had arrived at only with time and trouble. At other times I thought that it was wilful delusion, and that there could be no salvation possible for me. When I could think of nothing but of ending my days afflicted by these thoughts (which, far from weakening my trust in God, served only to increase my faith), I felt a sudden change come over me. My soul, which until then had been full of care and trouble, was now pervaded by a deep inner peace, as though it had arrived at its home, at a place of peace and rest.

Ever since that time, I have walked before God simply, in faith, with humility and with love, and taken diligent care to do nothing and think nothing which may displease Him. I hope that when I have done what I can, He will do with me what He pleases.

As for what I am now feeling, I cannot express it in words. I can know no pain or difficulty in my vocation, because I have no will but the will of God, which I try to bring about in everything I do. Indeed, I have submitted so entirely to it, that I would not pick up a straw from the ground if He had commanded me otherwise, or for any reason other than pure love for Him.

I have stopped practicing all devotions and set prayers except those which are required of me by my order. And I make it my only business to persevere in His holy presence. I keep myself in it by a simple, attentive state of mind, and, generally, by directing my thoughts fondly towards God. I think I can say that it is in these thoughts of affection that I find a real presence of God, or, to express myself better, an habitual, silent, and secret conversation between the soul and God. This conversation often causes me to be so transported with joy and rapture, inwardly and often also outwardly, that I am forced to moderate my emotions, and stop them becoming visible to others.

All in all, there is no doubt in my mind that my soul has been at one with God for these last thirty years and more. There are many things which I have passed over in my letter, so that it should not be tedious to you, but I think it proper to inform you how I consider myself before God, whom I know to be my King. I consider myself the most wretched man alive, full of blemishes and imperfections, and guilty of all sorts of crimes against my King. It is moved by a great sense of regret that I admit all my wickedness to Him, that I ask His forgiveness, and abandon myself to Him, place myself between His hands, so that He may do what He pleases with me. This King, full of mercy and goodness, far from chastising me, embraces me with love, makes me eat at His table, serves me with His own hands, and gives me the key to His treasures. He delights in keeping up a constant conversation with me, talking to me in a thousand ways, and treats me in every way as His favourite. This is how I consider myself from time to time in His holy presence.

My most usual method is this simple attentiveness, and this general, passionate direction of my thoughts towards God: indeed, I often feel a greater sweetness and delight in my attachment to Him than an infant feels at his mother's breast, so that if I may dare to use the expression, I should like to choose this state of mind, the 'bosom of God'. That is the closest I can come in words to describing the inexpressible sweetness that I feel and experience there. If my thoughts sometimes wander from that state, out of necessity or weakness, I am quickly called back to it by inner feelings, which are so charming and delightful, that I am ashamed to mention them. I hope that your reverence will think rather of my great wretchedness, of which I have told you everything, than on the great favours which God does me, unworthy and ungrateful of them as I am.

As for my set hours of prayer, they are nothing more than a continuation of the same exercise. Sometimes I consider myself there as a stone set before a sculptor to make a statue: this was how I presented myself to Him, wishing Him to make His perfect image in my soul, and make me exactly like Himself.

At other times, when I apply myself to prayer, I feel all my spirit and all my soul lift itself up, without any trouble or effort of my own, and it remains as if it were suspended and firmly fixed in God, its centre and place of rest.

I know that there are some who would attack me for this, saying that to indulge in this state of mind is to indulge in inactivity, delusion and self-love. I confess that it is a holy inactivity, and would be a happy self-love, if the soul were capable of it in that state, but it is not, because a soul in that state of repose cannot be disturbed from it by the acts it was previously used to: in the past, it was these acts which the soul depended on, but now they would hinder rather than help it.

Yet still I cannot bear to call this delusion, because the soul that enjoys God desires nothing but Him in this life. If this is a delusion in me, it is for God to remedy it. Let Him do what He pleases: I desire nothing but Him, and to be wholly devoted to Him.

You will, however, be obliged to send me your opinion, which I always receive with great deference, for I hold your reverence in great esteem.

I am yours in our Lord,

*I suppose he means that any idea he could have of God was unsatisfactory, because he saw that it was unworthy of God, and therefore his mind could only be satisfied by the view of God which is offered by faith, a view of God as infinite and incomprehensible, of God as He is in Himself, and not of how He can be conceived by human ideas.

THIRD LETTER

WRITTEN 12TH OCTOBER 1688

My Dearest Brother,

We have a God who is infinitely gracious, and knows all our wants. I always thought that He would reduce you to a state of crisis and misfortune. He will come in His own time, and when you least expect it. Hope in Him more than ever: thank Him for the favours he does you, particularly for the patience and strength He gives you in times of trouble. They are a clear sign of the care He takes of you, so comfort yourself with Him, and give thanks for all.

I also admire the strength and bravery of Mr. _____ . God has given him a good disposition, and a good mind: but there is still a little of the world, and a great deal of youth, in him. I hope the affliction which God sent him will cure him of this, and make him enter healthily into himself. It is an accident which is very appropriate to the purpose of engaging him to put all his trust in Him who accompanies him everywhere: let him think of Him as often as he can, especially in the times of greatest danger. A little lifting up of the heart is enough: just a little remembrance of God, just one act of inward worship, even when he is marching into battle, sword in hand-these are prayers which are acceptable to God, however short they may be, and far from weakening a soldier's courage in times of danger, they are what best serves to strengthen it.

Let him then think of God as much and as often as he can; let him grow gradually accustomed to this small but holy exercise; nobody will notice it, and nothing is easier than repeating these little internal devotions many times a day. Please advise him to think of God as much and as often as he can, and in the way described here: it is very befitting and most necessary for a soldier, who every day must face dangers which threaten his life, and often also his salvation. I hope that God will assist him and the family, and I am at their service should they need it: I am theirs and yours.

I am yours in our Lord,

FOURTH
LETTER

WRITTEN 1ST JUNE 1682

My Dearest Prioress,

You must know that, ever since he took religious orders more than forty years ago, his one constant concern has been to be always with God, and to do nothing, say nothing and think nothing which may displease Him; and he has desired this purely because he loves Him, and knows that He deserves infinitely more.

He is now so accustomed to the Divine presence, that he finds it never stops giving him relief, in every situation and through all his difficulties. For more than thirty years, his soul has never stopped being filled with joy, and his joy is often so great that he must make an effort to control it, and to stop it from being visible to others.

If he sometimes draws a little too far away from that Divine presence, God loses no time in calling him back to it by entering his soul and making Himself felt. This often happens at those times when he is busiest with other work. He is always completely faithful in answering these inner callings, whether by raising up his heart to God, or by looking meekly and fondly towards Him, or with such words as love finds for these occasions, such as " God, here I am, entirely devoted to you. Lord, make me as Your heart desires me to be." And then it seems to him (in fact he can feel it), that this God of love, who is satisfied with so few words, is again at rest, in the centre and depths of his soul. These experiences make him so certain that God is always at the depths or bottom of his soul, that there is nothing whatever which could ever make him doubt it.

Think what contentment and satisfaction he enjoys, from knowing he always has such a great treasure inside himself: he is no longer anxiously searching for it, but has it there waiting in front of him, so that he can take what he likes from it.

He frequently complains of our blindness, and often cries that we are to be pitied, we who content ourselves with so little. The treasure God has to bestow is infinite, he says, and we can pick it up with just a moment of thoughtful devotion. In our blindness, we hinder God, and stop His tide of graces from flowing freely. But when He finds a soul where a lively faith has taken root, He pours His graces and favours into that soul with abundance. Then they flow through that soul like a torrent, but this torrent is stopped from continuing outwards, and rather pours out its graces every which way, so that every last corner of the soul is flooded with countless graces.

Yet too often we stop this flood, by not giving it as much value as we ought to. But let us stop it no more: let us enter into and examine ourselves, find the bank that is stopping it, and break down that bank. Let us make way for grace; let us make up for lost time, because we may have only a little time left; let us be prepared for death, which cannot take long to catch up with us; because we only die once, and if we make a mistake then, there will be no chance to put it right later.

I say again, let us enter into and examine ourselves. There is no time to be lost: our souls are at stake. I believe that you have taken adequate measures, and should not be taken by surprise. I commend you for it, it is the one thing which is needed above all else: but we must, nevertheless, always work at it, because in spiritual life, not to progress is to go backwards. But those who are rocked by the breeze of the Holy Spirit move forward even when they are asleep. If the ship which is our soul is still tossed by other winds and storms, let us awake the Lord, who lies sleeping in it, and He will quickly calm the sea.

I have taken the liberty of communicating these good sentiments to you, so that you may compare them with your own: if you have had the misfortune (and God forbid, for it would be a great misfortune), that your own should have cooled off even slightly, I have no doubt that these will serve to kindle them again. Let us both recall, then, the first fervours of our youth. Let us profit from the example and sentiments of this brother: he is little known to the world, but known to God, and infinitely cherished by God. I will pray for you, and I ask that you keep me always in your prayers, I who am yours in the Lord.

I am yours in our Lord,

FIFTH LETTER

WRITTEN PRIOR TO NOVEMBER 1685

My Dear Prioress,

Today I received too books and a letter from Sister _____, who is preparing to take her vows, and who asks that your Order, and you yourself in particular, pray for her on this occasion. I can see that these prayers mean a good deal to her, and I beg you to make sure that she is not disappointed. Ask God to grant that she makes this sacrifice in light of his love alone, and with a firm resolution to dedicate herself entirely to Him. I will send you one of these books, which are concerned with the presence of God, a subject in which I believe the whole spiritual life is contained: it seems to me that whoever persists in practicing himself in this presence of God will soon become a spiritual person.

I know that, to practice it well, the soul must be emptied of everything else, because God wants to be the sole possessor of our hearts. Just as he cannot be the sole possessor of a heart which we have not first emptied of everything which is not Him, nor can He do as He wills unless we have left the space vacant for Him.

There is no sweeter and more delightful life in this world than a life of continual communion with God: that is something only those who practice it and experience it can understand. Yet still I advise you not to choose it with that motivation in mind.

It is not pleasure which we must look for in that exercise: we must do it according to a principle of love, and because God wishes to possess us.

If I were a preacher, I would preach, above all else, the practice of the presence of God, and if I were a spiritual adviser, it is that which I would advise to everyone, as I believe so strongly that it is necessary, and easy at the same time.

Ah, if only we knew how much we need the grace and assistance of God, we would never lose sight of Him, not even for a moment. Believe me, and make an immediate, firm and sacred vow that you will never willingly forget God, and that you will spend the rest of your days in His holy presence, depriving yourself, if He sees fit, of all consolations out of your love for Him.

Set about this work with all your heart, and rest assured that, if you do it as you should, you will soon feel the benefits of it. I will help you with my prayers, poor as they are. I ask that you remember me in your prayers and recommend me to those of your order: I am theirs and, most particularly, yours.

I am yours in our Lord,

SIXTH LETTER

WRITTEN 3RD NOVEMBER 1685

My Dearest Prioress,

I have received from Mrs. _____ the things which you gave her for me. I am surprised that you have not given me your thoughts on that little book which I sent you and which you must have received. Please, I beg you, apply yourself, with all your heart and soul, to practicing what it teaches, in your old age: it is better late than never.

I cannot imagine how religious people can live with satisfaction, without the practice of the presence of God. As for myself, I live retired from the world, and, as much as I can, keeping Him in the depths and centre of my soul. And while I am with Him, I fear nothing, but the slightest movement away from Him is unbearable.

This exercise is not very tiring for the body. It is still good, however, to deprive it, from time to time, of many little pleasures which in themselves are innocent and lawful, because God will not allow a soul which wants to dedicate itself entirely to Him to find pleasures in other things than in Him: that is more than reasonable.

I do not mean by that that we ought to impose a brutal constraint on ourselves. No, we must serve God in a state of holy liberty, we must do our work faithfully, without troubling or disquieting ourselves, bringing our spirit gently and calmly back to God whenever we find it straying from Him. It is necessary, though, to rid ourselves of all troubles and cares, and even of a good many particular forms of devotion, good in themselves, but which are often approached in the wrong way, because in fact these devotions are only means to an end. If then, by this exercise of the presence of God, we are with He who is our end, it is useless for us to go back to the means: rather, we can continue our exchange of love with Him, remaining in His holy presence, now with an act of submission, now with an act of praise, or adoration, or desire, or thanksgiving, and in every way our spirit can think of.

Do not be discouraged if you find, in your body, a reluctance for this exercise: you must force yourself to continue. One often thinks, at first, that it is time wasted, but you must carry on with it, and be quite determined to persevere in these things until death, despite all the difficulties which can arise.

I ask you to pray for me, and to recommend me to the prayers of your whole order.

I am yours in our Lord,

SEVENTH
LETTER
WRITTEN DURING 1689

My Dearest Lady,

I feel very sorry for you. It will be of great importance to you if you can leave the care of your affairs to _____, and spend the rest of your life adoring God. He does not ask any great things from us, but only that you remember Him, that you adore Him, that you offer him a prayer to receive His blessing; that at other times you offer Him your pains, or give Him thanks for the favours He has done you and which He still does you, in the midst of your troubles; and that you come to Him for comfort as often as you can. Raise your heart up to Him, even during your meals and when you are in the company of others. You do not need to shout very loudly: He is nearer to us than we think, and there is no need to be constantly in church to be with God—we can make our heart an oratory in which to retreat to speak with God in submission, humility and love. Everyone can have these private talks with God, some more often, others less: He knows what we are capable of. So let us start. Perhaps He is only waiting for a good resolution from us. Let us gather our courage. We only have a little time left to live: you will soon be sixty-four, and I am almost eighty. Let us live and die with God. The worst torments will be sweet and pleasant if we are with Him, while the greatest pleasures would be a cruel punishment for us without Him. May He be blessed for all! Amen.

Become accustomed in this way, little by little, to adoring Him, to asking His pardon, to offering Him your heart from time to time, when you are in the middle of your work, and even at any moment when you can.

Do not stick fastidiously to certain rules or to particular forms of devotion, but live in your confidence in God, and act with love and humility. You can count on my poor prayers for _____, and reassure them that I am their servant in our Lord.

I am yours in our Lord,

EIGHTH
LETTER
WRITTEN ON AN UNKNOWN DATE.

Dear Madame,

You tell me nothing new: you are not the only one to be distracted, in your prayers, by thoughts you have of other things. Our mind is naturally prone to wander greatly, but as our will controls all our faculties, we must use it to call them back, and to bring them back to God, who is their ultimate end. When our mind, having not been sufficiently disciplined by the contemplation and reflection of our first years of devotion, has picked up some bad habits of distraction and unruliness, it is very difficult to root them out, and normally they lead us, even against our will, to the things of this world.

I believe that a cure for this is to confess our faults and to humble ourselves before God. I would advise that you do not use a great mass of words in your prayers, as words and long speeches can often be a source of distraction. Stand in prayer before God, as a mute, paralysed beggar before a rich man's house. May your first care be to keep your mind in the presence of the Lord. If sometimes it strays and is lost far away from Him, do not let this cause you too many worries: trouble and disquiet serve only to distract the mind further, and not to help collect it. You must simply turn back to God with your will, and if you persevere like this, God will have pity on you.

A sure way of keeping your mind calm and collected in times

of prayer is not to let it wander away at other times: you must keep it always strictly in the presence of God. Like this your mind will grow used to thinking of Him often, and you will find it easy to keep it calm during the time for prayer, or at least to call it back, if it becomes distracted.

I have already told you, at length, in my previous letters, of the advantages we can draw from this practice of the presence of God: let us then apply ourselves seriously too it and pray the one for the other.

I am yours in our Lord,

NINTH
LETTER
WRITTEN 28TH MARCH 1689

My Dearest Madame,

The enclosed is a reply to the letter I have received from _____: please be good enough as to give it to her. She seems to me to be someone who is full of good will, but she wants to move faster than God's grace. It takes more than a day to become holy. I commend her to your care. We must help one another with our advice and our good example. I will be obliged to you if you could give me news of her from time to time and tell me whether she is as devout and obedient as she needs to be?

Let us remind ourselves that our only duty in this life is to please God and that everything besides that is mere vanity and folly. You and I have lived in the religious, that is the monastic, life, for around forty years.

Have we used these years to love and to serve God, who has called us to this state and for that end? I am full of shame and confusion when I reflect, on the one hand on the great favours God has done me and continues to do me, and on the other of how badly I have used them and of how little progress I have made towards perfection.

Since, in His mercy, He gives us still a little more time, let us set to work with sincerity, make up for lost time, turn back in complete confidence to the merciful Father who is always ready to receive us with affection. Let us renounce, generously renounce, out of love for Him, everything which is not Him: He is worthy of infinitely more. Let us think of Him constantly. Let us put all our trust in Him. I do not doubt that we will soon feel the effects in receiving the abundance of His grace. With that grace, we can do anything, and without it, we can do nothing but sin.

We cannot escape the dangers which are so common in life without God's immediate and constant aid: let us ask for it constantly. How can we pray to Him without being in Him? And how can we be in Him without thinking of Him often? And how can we think of Him often if not by developing a holy habit?

You will tell me that I am always repeating the same thing. That is true, because it is the best and easiest method I know, and as I do not use any other method, I recommend it to everyone. We must know someone before we can love them. To know God, we must think of Him often, and when we come to love Him, then too we will think of Him often, because our heart will be where our treasure is. There is an argument worthy indeed of our consideration.

I am yours in our Lord,

TENTH LETTER

WRITTEN 29TH OCTOBER 1689

Dearest Lady,

I have found it very difficult to bring myself to write to Mr. _____ and I do so now purely because you and Mrs _____ want me to. Please address the letter and send it to him. I am very happy about the trust you have in God, and hope that He will increase it in you more and more: we cannot have too much trust in such a good and loyal friend who will abandon us neither in this world nor in the next.

If Mr. _____ takes advantage of the loss he has suffered and puts all his trust in God, God will soon give him another, still better friend. He arranges hearts as he sees fit.

Perhaps Mr. _____ was too fond of the friend he lost. We must love our friends, but without letting this love encroach upon our love for God, who must always hold the first place in our affections.

Remember, I beg you, the advice which I have given you, that is to think of God often, day and night, when you are busy working and even during your times of rest: He is always close to you and with you. Do not leave Him on His own. You would not dare to leave a friend who came to visit you on his own: why then should God be neglected? Do not forget Him, but think of Him often, adore Him continually, live and die in Him: that is the glorious occupation of a Christian. What is more, it is there that our treasure lies: if we do not know that, we must learn it. I will do all I can to help you with my prayers.

I am yours in our Lord,

ELEVENTH
LETTER
WRITTEN 17ᵀᴴ NOVEMBER 1690

My Dear Friend,

I do not pray for you to be relieved of your suffering, but I sincerely pray to God that He will give you the strength and the patience to bear them for as long as He pleases. Take strength in He who holds you fastened to the Cross. He will untie you when he sees fit. Happy are those who suffer with Him! Make yourself accustomed to suffering in that way, and seek in Him the strength to bear as much as he deems necessary for you, and for as long as he deems it to be necessary.

People of good society do not understand these truths, and this should not surprise us, because they suffer as people of society do, and not as Christians do. They regard illness as an affliction for the body and not as a favour from God, and seeing it only in this light, they find in it nothing but grief and hurt. But those who receive illness from the hand of God and who see it as the result of His mercy and as the means He employs for their salvation, they usually find in it a great comfort and a real consolation.

I wish you could convince yourself that God is often (in a certain sense) closer to us, and has a more real presence within us, in sickness than in health. Do not rely on any other doctor, for it is my belief that He keeps the task of curing you for Himself. Put then all your trust in Him, and you will soon reap the rewards in your recovery, a recovery which we often delay by putting our trust in remedies rather than in God.

Whatever remedies you take, they will only work insofar as He will allow them to. When suffering comes to us from God, He alone can cure it. He often sends illnesses of the body to save us from illnesses of the soul. Take comfort in the supreme doctor of the body and of the soul. I can tell what you will say to me: you will say that I am saying this from a position of great comfort, and that I am eating and drinking my fill at our Lord's Table. You are right in this, but do you think it would be a little matter for the greatest criminal in the world to eat at God's table, and be served by Him, and yet despite this not to know that he had been forgiven? I think his unease would be great that nothing could assuage it, except for his trust in the goodness of his Sovereign. So I assure you that, however much pleasure I may taste at the table of my King, I am always tormented by my sins, which are always present before my eyes, and tormented also because I do not know whether they can be forgiven: in reality, though, those torments themselves give me pleasure.

Be satisfied with the condition in which God has put you. However happy I may seem to you, I envy you. Pain and suffering would be a paradise for me, if I suffered with God, and the greatest of pleasures would be a Hell, if I could enjoy them without Him: my only consolation would be to endure something for Him.

I must soon leave you to talk with God. What delights me in this life, is that I can see Him by the light of faith, and I see Him so clearly that I could sometimes say "I no longer believe, but I see." I can feel what faith teaches us and, in this confidence and this practice of the faith, I want to live and die in Him.

So never stop persevering with God: He is the only possible help and the only possible comfort for your suffering, and I will beg Him to be with you. I give you my best wishes.

I am yours in our Lord,

TWELFTH LETTER

WRITTEN 28TH NOVEMBER 1690

My Dear Friend,

If we were better accustomed to practicing the presence of God, we would find that it made any physical illness much easier to bear. God often allows us to suffer a little, in order to purify our souls and to oblige us to persevere with Him.

Gather your courage, never stop offering Him your pains, ask Him for the strength to endure them. Above all, develop the habit of talking with God often, and of forgetting Him as little as possible. Adore Him in your frailties, offer yourself to Him from time to time and, in your moments of greatest suffering, beg Him humbly and affectionately (as a child begs his father) to make you conform to His holy will. I will try to help you with my humble prayers.

God has many ways of drawing us closer to Him. Sometimes, He hides from us, but at these times we must call on the aid of that one thing which will not fail us in our hour of need, faith, and it is on faith that we must base our trust, and all this trust must be in God. I do not know how God will deal with me: I am always happy. The whole world suffers, yet I, who deserve the strictest punishment, feel a joy so continual and so great that I can hardly contain it.

I would willingly ask God to let me share in your hardships, if it were not for my weakness, which is so great that if he left me on my own even for one moment, I would be the most wretched man alive. And yet I cannot see how God could leave me, for faith gives me the conviction that He never abandons us, unless it is us who abandon Him first. Let us be afraid of leaving Him. Let us always be with Him. Let us live and die in His holy presence. Do you pray for me as I pray for you?

I am yours in our Lord,

THIRTEENTH
LETTER
WRITTEN 21ST DECEMBER 1690

My Dearest Friend,

It pains me to see you suffer for so long: what comforts me, and makes me look on your pains in a happier light, is that they are a proof of God's love for you. Look at them like this and you will find them easier to bear. It is my view that yours is a case where you should leave human remedies to one side, and give yourself up entirely to God's providence. Perhaps all he is waiting for to cure you is that resignation, and a perfect trust in Him. Since, despite all the troubles you have gone to, medicine has proved powerless and your illness is growing still worse, you will not be putting God to the test if you abandon yourself into his arms, and wait for Him to do everything.

I have told you, in my last letter, that he sometimes allows illnesses of the body, so as to cure illnesses of the soul. Have courage then. Make a virtue of necessity. Ask God, not to release you from your pains, but to give you the strength to bear them resolutely, out of love for Him, for as long as He pleases.

Such prayers are, it is true, hard on the body, but for this they are all the more pleasing to God, and all the sweeter for those who love Him. Love lightens pain, and when one loves God, one suffers, out of love for Him, with joy and courage. I beg you to do the same: comfort yourself with Him who is the doctor for every illness. He is the Father of the afflicted, always ready to come to their aid. He loves us infinitely more than we think: let us then love Him, and not seek consolation elsewhere. I hope that you will soon receive this consolation. Farewell. I will help you with my prayers, poor as they are, and will always be yours in our Lord,

FOURTEENTH
LETTER
WRITTEN 22ND JANUARY 1691

My Dearest Friend,

I rend thanks to our Lord that He has relieved you a little, as you wished Him to. I have often been close to death, but I have never been as happy as I am now. And so I have not prayed for my pain to be relieved, but for the strength to suffer with courage, humility and love. Ah, how sweet it is to suffer with God! However great our suffering may be, let us receive it with love. It is Heaven to suffer with Him, so that if we want to enjoy the peace of Heaven in this life, we must become accustomed to conversing with Him with humility, intimacy and affection. We must stop our minds from wandering from Him in any circumstances, make our hearts a spiritual temple where we continually adore Him, keep constant guard over ourselves so as to do, say or think nothing which may displease Him. When our minds are thus occupied with thoughts of God, suffering becomes full of sweetness and comfort.

I know that, to arrive at this state, the starting point is very difficult, because we must act purely out of faith. But we also know that we can do anything by the grace of God, that God never refuses those who ask Him with sincerity. Knock at His door, persevere in your knocking. I can vouch for it that He will open it when the time comes and that He will grant you all at once what

He deferred giving you for years. Farewell. Pray to Him for me as I pray to Him for you. I hope to see Him soon.

I am yours in our Lord,

FIFTEENTH
LETTER
WRITTEN 6TH FEBRUARY 1691

My Dearest Friend,

God knows better for us what is good for us, and everything He does is for our benefit. If we knew how much He loves us, we would always be ready to receive from him the bitter with the sweet: everything which comes from Him would be pleasing to us. The most painful afflictions seem unbearable to us only when we look at them in a false light. When we see them bestowed by the hand of God, when we know that it is our loving Father who humiliates us and causes us to suffer, our torments will lose their bitterness and will become rather a comfort for us.

Let us put all our efforts into seeking to know God: the more we know Him, the more we will want to know Him. As love is usually in proportion to knowledge, the greater and more profound our knowledge is, greater too will be our love, and if our love for God is great, we will love Him as much in our pains as in our pleasures.

Let us not waste our time seeking or loving God for the perceptible favours He has done us, or may do us. Such favours, however high and magnificent they may be, can never bring us as close to God as a simple act of faith. Let us seek Him often through faith. He is within us: let us not look for Him elsewhere. Would we not be guilty and worthy of blame if we loved Him only for trifles which do not please Him and which He may well be offended by? It is to be feared that these trifles will one day cost us dear. Let us dedicate ourselves to Him, with all our hearts, from this moment onwards. Let us remove from our hearts everything which is not Him: He wants to be our sole possessor. Ask Him this favour. If, for our part, we do everything we can, we will soon feel the change we yearned after take place within us. I cannot thank Him enough for the relief He has granted you. I wait for Him to grant me, in His mercy, the favour of letting me see Him in a few days' time.[1] Let us pray for one another.

I am yours in the Lord,

---

1 He was confined to his bed two days later, and died on Monday, February 12, 1691, at 9.00 AM.

About the Author

Mark Bilton BSc. GradDipBus. MBA. FAICD. FAIM

Mark Bilton is a, "Change Catalyst" with extensive Managing Director and CEO experience. He has led business transformation in many companies including, Gloria Jean's Coffees' global business, as Group Managing Director overseeing 40 countries.

Mark has led transformational change in many sectors, including importing, wholesale and retail. His leadership experience spans diverse industries; coffee, textiles, garments, appliances and consumer electronics.

He is internationally recognized for excellence in 'Change Management'. In 2011 he was awarded the "Young President's Organization's" prestigious "Terry Plochman Award" for global "Best of the Best". In 2014 he received the Michael Page 'Australian Retail Executive Award'.

Mark has served as an Independent Director on numerous 'not for profit', industry, leadership and commercial boards.

Mark has a passion for Christians in Business, and is the founder of 'Called to Business', who "encourage and equip Christians to be effective at work". He is also a speaker and the author of many books including "Monday Matters: Finding God in Your Workplace."

He is married to Helen, has three teenage children and lives in Sydney, Australia.

Recommended Resources

Called to Business: www.CalledtoBusiness.com

Mark Bilton's online ministry to "Encourage and Equip Christians to be effective at Work." You will find many resources in this ministry, including a powerful weekly biblical business e-message that you can receive in your e-mail.

You can find *Called to Business* on the social media sites listed below:

www.Facebook.com/CalledtoBusiness

www.Twitter.com/Calledto

Mark Bilton: www.MarkBilton.com

Founder of *Called to Business*' Mark Bilton's personal blog.

You can find Mark Bilton on the social media sites listed below:

www.Facebook.com/MarkBilton

www.Twitter.com/MarkBilton

www.Linkedin/in/MarkBilton

www.YouTube.com/MarkBilton

www.Google.com/+MarkBilton

Other Recommended Marketplace Ministries.

www.MarketplaceLeaders.org

Os Hillman is president of Marketplace Leaders, an organization whose purpose is to help men and women discover and fulfill God's complete purposes through their work and to view their work as ministry. Marketplace Leaders exists to help men and women fulfill God's call on their lives by providing a *free* devotional that goes out to over a quarter of a million people all over the world and by training business leaders to see their work as a catalyst for change through training events and other ministry events.

www.LICC.org.uk

LICC exists to envision and equip Christians and their churches for whole-life missionary discipleship in the world. They seek to serve them with biblical frameworks, practical resources, training, and models so that they flourish as followers of Jesus and grow as whole-life disciple-making communities. Mark Greene is one of the most articulate and effective communicators in the marketplace today.

www.GodatWork.org.uk

In his book *God at Work*, Ken Costa writes about how the Christian faith should and can be lived out in day-to-day life at work. As a high-profile banker in the city of London, he considers the challenges of living out his faith at work and speaks openly of his own struggles with ambition, money, relationships, success, and failure.

By using the Biblical principles that underpin his faith and applying them to the 21st-century workplace of today, he offers practical advice on tackling the common problems familiar to many: the work-life balance, stress, ambition, failure, and disappointment.

www.BusinessasMissionNetwork.com
This is the most comprehensive source of information about the Business as Mission Movement, with many links to numerous companies, resources, and articles.

www.EdSilvoso.com
Ed Silvoso is one of the most effective marketplace ministers in the world, transforming many businesses and lives as he teaches comprehensively in many countries.

www.JohnMaxwell.com
John Maxwell is still one of the best and most-respected experts and teachers on leadership and personal growth.

Other books by Mark Bilton.

MON**DAY**
memos

A daily devotional for those in the workplace.

By Mark Bilton

Does God really have a plan and a purpose for my work?

God is vitally, passionately, and intimately interested in the workplace. Many have embraced the biblical concept of our whole life being impacted by God, and that there is no separation between the sacred and the secular.

How do you integrate your faith with your work? Through real commercial experience, author Mark Bilton has walked with God and seen Him open doors that have taken him from the shop floor to the boardroom; from sales assistant to CEO.

In this book are 365 short, sharp, insightful messages that are scriptural and applicable to you and your work. They will transform your work life, and your workplace. There is no inconsistency between a Christian worldview and commercial success.

Work is a vital part of His plan and purpose for us. We have been lovingly crafted, anointed and appointed, for a particular purpose. We will only reach our full potential as we recognise God's hand at work in our work.

www.**MondayMemos**.com

MON DAY
matters

Finding God in your workplace.

By Mark Bilton

Is God really interested in my work?

There is a revolution taking place around the world. It is a realization that God is vitally, passionately, and intimately interested in the workplace. Many have embraced the biblical concept of our whole lives being impacted by God and that there is no separation between the sacred and the secular.

How do you find God in your workplace? In this book, Mark provides insights and a practical framework that lays out God's purpose for work. These lessons have been mined from real world commercial experience. Author Mark Bilton has walked with God and seen Him open doors that have taken him from the shop floor to the boardroom; from sales assistant to CEO.

Work is a vital part of His plan and purpose for us. We have been lovingly crafted, anointed, and appointed for a particular purpose. We will only reach our full potential as we recognize God's hand at work in our work.

www.**MondayMatters**.net

77 PROVERBS
FOR LEADERS

A CONTEMPORARY VERSION OF THE 'BOOK OF PROVERBS' WITH LEADERSHIP INSIGHTS

BY MARK BILTON

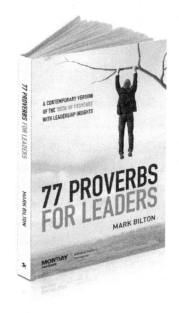

Leadership can be a rewarding but sometimes isolating experience. All leaders need input and wisdom. Whether you are a business owner, commercial leader or aspire to be one, this book is for you.

The writer of most of 'Proverbs', King Solomon, is considered the wisest man who ever lived; he certainly was one of the wealthiest. His name is synonymous with wisdom.

The 'Book of Proverbs' is considered by Jews and Christians to be the inspired word of God. Interspersed within this contemporary translation are 77 Leadership Messages by experienced CEO, Mark Bilton. The wisdom in '77 Proverbs' will equip you to be an effective leader.

www.**77proverbs**.com

CPSIA information can be obtained
at www.ICGtesting.com
Printed in the USA
BVOW10s0615070816

458212BV00021B/516/P

9 780987 339843